ALSO BY BROOKS HAXTON

Poetry

Nakedness, Death, and the Number Zero
The Sun at Night
Traveling Company
Dead Reckoning
Dominion
The Lay of Eleanor and Irene

Translations

Fragments: The Collected Wisdom of Heraclitus
Dances for Flute and Thunder: Praises, Prayers, and Insults
Victor Hugo: Selected Poems

UPROAR

UPROAR
Antiphonies to Psalms

Poems by Brooks Haxton

 Alfred A. Knopf   New York   2006

THIS IS A BORZOI BOOK
PUBLISHED BY ALFRED A. KNOPF

www.randomhouse.com/knopf/poetry

Library of Congress Cataloging-in-Publication Data
Haxton, Brooks [date]
Uproar : antiphonies to Psalms : poems / by
Brooks Haxton.—1st ed.
p. cm.
ISBN 0-375-71016-7 (pbk)
1. Religious poetry, American. I. Title.
PS3558.A825U95 2004
811'.54—dc22   2003060477

Manufactured in the United States of America
Published April 19, 2004
First Paperback Edition, March 14, 2006

To my father

Kenneth Haxton

1919–2002

for his love

and art and learning

Contents

Preface: Lying about God

The psalms my mother had me learn as a boy were no longer the songbook of her faith, but they were poems her people handed down to her, and she to me, to keep and pass along.

My mother's mother quoted from both Testaments, chapter and verse. Her father, in his work as a petroleum distributor, used to travel with Bibles in the trunk of his Cadillac and hand them out to hitch-hikers and to inmates in the Louisiana jails where he led prayers along the way.

After my mother grew up and left the Presbyterian Church, she read aloud to my brothers and me from the King James. As a writer of fiction, though agnostic, she still felt the power of the Book and had us memorize "The Lord is my shepherd" and "I will lift up mine eyes unto the hills."

My father's family was less strict in their religion. Before World War I, my father's father made all-American playing football for Ole Miss, which must have been a religious experience, much as dancing was for his wife. She studied with a follower of Isadora Duncan, and danced barefoot on the stage of the People's Theater in Greenville, Mississippi, her hometown. Maybe she took to heart the last two psalms where they say, "Let them praise his name in the dance" and "Praise him with the timbrel and dance." Her rabbi denounced her from the pulpit, nevertheless, and her whole family left the temple. She and some of her Jewish friends became Episcopalians, but she never paid much mind to Judaism or Christianity.

Music was what moved her. Though she took my father as a boy to the St. James Episcopal Church, he became an atheist. Still, he valued Hebrew scripture, and his magnum opus, from more than a hundred musical compositions, is an oratorio about the life of Moses, with a libretto adapted from the King James by my mother. He requested that no service be held at his funeral, but one of his best friends, a rabbi, spoke at the graveside.

A few years back, when I was translating ancient Greek poems from the same period as the Hebrew Psalter, I began to feel that I wanted my own poems to flow from sources as vital to me as Aphrodite and Apollo were to the Greeks. I turned to the Psalms as poems from my childhood, from my parents' and their parents' childhoods, with this kind of charge. Psalms had fascinated me before I understood what such old-fashioned language meant, and later, when I learned the meanings of the words, the poems fascinated me and moved me that much more.

Still, my return to them is doubtful. In the sixties, distrustful of groups and faiths, I left home an atheist. Never quite a flower child, I did once hand out dandelions to racists and hawks. They understood, and found this as infuriating as I had hoped. Meanwhile, the atheism I professed was no less facile than the conventional beliefs I meant to oppose.

At college, where I had been reading about myth and religion, an old woman, a stranger, seeing me caught up in a performance of Handel's *Messiah*, asked if I were Christian, and I found myself saying for the first time that I was. I called myself a Christian for about ten years, while trying to absorb what this meant. Without joining a church, I kept reading, and my confusion deepened.

I stopped calling myself a Christian because the promiscuity of my beliefs made the label seem wrong. My wife calls herself a Jew, though she has never been preoccupied with religious experience. Even when she was a Quaker, she was a Jew. Her people have been

Jews for thousands of years. For me, this clarity is bracing, and I am grateful that our children can grow up as Jews.

When I started writing these poems, I was reading scripture in a study group with rabbis and scholars; my son, Isaac, was studying to be a bar mitzvah. He and his younger sisters, Lillie and Miriam, read Hebrew with understanding. They know prayers by heart. They revere the Torah, although Isaac, like his father's mother long ago, has become agnostic as a teenager.

Religious writings have described the experience of people in so many times and places that not to believe in any of them seems gratuitous. I might as well choose not to believe in Bach's cello suites, or in the imagination that informs them, or in the connection between music and the cosmos where it occurs. Being is beyond belief.

The polymorphous soul of my imagination keeps returning to the gods of ancient Egypt, Greece, and India. My theological yearnings gravitate toward Buddhism. But I observe even my home religions from outside.

When I kept a journal of dreams, I found as I remembered more that any record of a dream seemed inexact. The same is true of my unorthodox experience of God. It would be a lie to say that I believe in God, and it would be another lie to say that I do not. To step back from these warring impulses and to say I do not know feels almost true, but less true, maybe, than convenient. In these antiphonies the fictions find beyond the lies, approximations, and conveniences an intensity of engagement with the contradictions of experience.

Rival orthodoxies make free with religious traditions while disagreeing among themselves and keeping the admittedly confused soul shut outside. In my confusion, I need as much as any rabbi or priest to dwell on revelations of the soul's yearning and faith, rage and exultation. The faiths I have inherited—and the attendant doubts—are mine, and I am theirs, whether we choose each other or not.

Part of me still wants to stir things up by giving people weeds that I call flowers. With luck, my readers and I can see past this into the challenge of letting the Psalms, like any art that matters, find us where we live. Inattention to great poetry is a loss of soul, whether the inattention cloaks itself in conventional approval or in programmatic opposition.

The psalmists have expressed so many ways of thinking and feeling, at the king's court, on the field of battle, in the temple and the house of bondage, that I take psalms less as doctrine than as outcries, and I cry back in these poems from whatever vantage I can find.

To my mind, dogmas that turn us away from our most searching engagement with scripture are like owl's eyes on the wings of a moth—effective in a way, impressive, glinting in the darkness, beautiful in the light, but not, when we examine them, as they have been made to appear.

A Note on Sources

Reading the King James Version of Psalms in tandem with these poems might appear more relevant where I have echoed the sense of the psalm quoted, less so where I have reacted against it, and not at all where I have spun off into associations largely unrelated to the psalm. But all of these antiphonies, to my mind, speak as answering voices through their various masks: atheist, devotionalist, agnostic, child, lover, husband, friend, parent, and citizen. A few of these masks suggest fictional or historical characters. Notes at the end of the book mention some of the sources.

UPROAR

I cried unto God with my voice . . .

Thy way is in the sea, and thy path in the great waters, and thy footsteps are not known.

PSALM 77

SUBMERSIBLE

Why art thou cast down, O my soul?   Psalm 42

Down from twilight into dark at noon,
through darker, down until the black
could not be more devoid of star
or sunlight, O my soul, near freezing
in subphotic stillness past
the fragile strands of glowing jelly
radiant with tentacles to sting,
and bioluminescent lures of anglers,
down where water beading on the cold hatch
overhead has sheathed in dewdrops
the titanium, past dragonfish
with night-lights set into their heads
and flanks, past unlit cruisers,
blackcod, owl fish, eelpout, skate,
where spider crabs, arms long as mine,
on creamy prongs drift floodlit
over the pillow lava, here,
our craft has taken us where no one
could have come till now but corpses.

I AM

*And he hath put a new song in my mouth, even
praise unto our God.*   Psalm 40

The fog I call the world is not a cloud of atoms
only, but a cloud of feelings, and ideas. I mind
my little bumps. I grieve. I think about non-being.
All I do is what my flesh can do, yet everything
my flesh can do feels strange. I am the swelling
of a salt sea onto an armature of chalk, the calm
of a tidal pool where brain cells live, the wind,
the lightning storm where thought flares into thought.
I taste damp sparks inside my tongue. If sayings
gather under the name of Faith, or Art, I let them
when they let me let them, and my mind clears.

APOLLO 12

Here, in the xeroxed panorama on my desk, a man
is crouching slightly in his spacesuit, leaning
forward, hands swung up, as though about to leap.
The sun behind him hangs at the horizon.
His long shadow lies before him, shadow-toe
to toe of lunar overshoe, in several-billion-
year-old regolithic dust. This is the Known
Sea, where at the half-moon one leap from the light
edge carries a man some distance into the dark.
The man, whose face hid under the visor almost
everybody has forgotten, in this picture, thirty
years ago, is young: he is about to leap for joy.

THY NAME

My God, my God, why hast thou forsaken me? . . . I
will declare thy name unto my brethren.   Psalm 22

OK. Let's not call what ditched us God:
ghu, the root in Sanskrit, means not God
but only the calling thereupon. Let's call God
Fun. In the beginning was the Word, and the Word
was Fun. Fun created man in his own image.
The fool hath said in his heart, There is no Fun.
Let's call the House of God the Funhouse. Fun
derives, according to Dr. Onions (may he
with his Johnson rest in peace), from fond,
or foolish. God, in this prime sense, is fond
of us, and we, if all goes well, of him. Let's
call God luck. There is no luck in scripture.
Chance gets mentioned several times, my favorite
being, Time and chance happeneth to them all;
but luck is the unspoken name. King David
to the harp and sackbut sings, in paraphrase, My luck?
Gimme a fucking break! With my luck, how do I know?

WEDDING SONG

*All thy garments smell of myrrh, and aloes, and
cassia, out of the ivory palaces, whereby they
have made thee glad.*   Psalm 45

Daughter of the king of Tyre, your queen,
I come to you the king of Judah—mine
and yours, the glories of the kingdoms. Here,
my outward garment is gold thread and silk,
beneath it linen laced with needlework.
Behold, my Lord, and breathe the cinnamom
and camphor, orrisroot and aniseed, crushed
lavender. My sheen is oils and essences
of fragrant wood and spices. Lord, I come,
your queen, in jewels. In gold chains: a girl
could rend one with her smallest finger.
We two join the kingdoms in a cloud of incense.
Listen: at our door three handmaids sing
for us the praises of Our Lady Ashtart.

TIME MAY STAY

Time may stay but never
stop. The flower blooming
out of the swollen fruit.
The river flowing
under a glazen skin.
Planets after sunset wander
where the last few swallows
dodge the first few bats.

UNCLEAN

*I am like a pelican of the wilderness: I am like
an owl of the desert. I watch, and am as a sparrow
alone upon the house top.*   Psalm 102

The pelican in scripture is unclean. It pukes dead fish
onto the hatchlings, and it roosts alone, like Satan
on the Tree of Life. Nobody told me. I liked pelicans.
I liked owls, too. I used to lie awake and listen,
wanting to become an owl, to fly, to see through darkness,
turn my head and look straight back behind me. I was
happy, as kids go, but I did not belong in human form.
Sparrows peck grain from fresh dung. In this world rich
means filthy. Leopardi, in his high Romantic musings
on the sparrow, does not say the poet is a shitbird, just
that, singing by himself, he acts like one, and wishes
he could feel more like one, unashamed to do so. Here,
the preacher (burning in his bones with fever, puking
half-digested fish, and hooting, sleepless in the ruins
like the baleful dead) cries: O Lord, take me not away.

DARK

The night also is thine.   Psalm 74

The darkest night I ever saw
I bleeped the car light on
from my front stoop
and couldn't see my feet
to take a step. A fog, at least,
you'd see. But this was just
thick dark. Headlights
disappeared. And from the car
the house with every window lit
looked empty as an open grave.

I WOKE UP AND IT WAS TIME

4 a.m., August 11, 2001

I have loved the habitation of thy house.   Psalm 26

I woke up on the couch a little drunk,
already stumbling to the john, where I stood
grateful for the warm swoon of the animal
I am. Watching the stream reminded me
about the shooting stars. The night air
after a few days' record heat felt godsent.
Barefoot in the dew, I wheeled my lawn chair
under the half-moon into the hemlock's shadow
by the gate. Tree crickets were singing.
Three bright streaks came out of the east
and faded into the Little Bear, three
in an hour. The crickets hushed. Day
broke, and sparrows sang me back to sleep.

EVERY DEATH IS MAGIC FROM
THE ENEMY TO BE AVENGED

Lest mine enemy say, I have prevailed against him;
and those that trouble me rejoice when I am moved.
Psalm 13

When fever burned the last light out of my daughter's eyes,
I swore to find and kill the ones to blame. Men
must mount the long boat in the dark with spears.
At dawn, where the flowering spicebush hid my scent,
I crouched. A young wife, newborn slung across her chest,
came first for springwater. She stooped. My god,
for vengeance, spoke her secret name inside my ear. Her god
stepped back with no scream, his right hand at his mouth,
the knuckles clenched between the pointed teeth.

1985

The righteous shall rejoice when he seeth the
vengeance; he shall wash his feet in the blood of
the wicked.   Psalm 58

It was the fortieth year since Buchenwald: two thousand
Jewish refugees in Sudan starved while Reagan visited
the graves of Nazis. CBS paid off Westmoreland
for their rude disclosure of his lies and crimes:
he *had* killed thirty of the enemy, let's not forget,
for every one lost us: he was owed something.
That year, though, no terrorist could touch God's work
in Mexico and north of Bogotá: an earthquake here,
volcano there, and numbers do not signify the dead,
each corpse incomprehensible as to the widow Klinghoffer
her Leon, shot, dumped overboard as if to make a point.
Westmoreland said the Viet Cong could be identified
from the attacking aircraft as all personnel in uniform
below. Their uniform, he told us, was the native dress.

KINGLINESS

Who is this King of glory?   Psalm 24

Richard the Third, in prudent scholarship,
is rehabilitated. Murdering the children,
come to think of it, was not so bad.
Any king, they say, would understand.

PRAISE YE HIM

*Shall the dust praise thee? shall it declare thy
truth?* Psalm 30

Two hundred Philistines he slew,
and stripped their foreskins
as a dowry for Saul's daughter
Michal, opening the snare between
whose thighs he entered the succession.

Let them be as cut in pieces, David sang,
his fingers nimble on the strings. Thy foot
be dipped in blood, he wished King Saul,
and the tongue of thy dogs in the same.

David twice stood over Saul asleep.
He spared the king his father twice,
and on Saul's throne at last he sang:
For God is my defence, and the God
of my mercy: praise ye him:
his enemies shall lick the dust.

DIALECTIC

For they speak not peace . . .   Psalm 35

The mockingbird in the sour cherry
next door sang, All mine,
all mine. So I said, Yours?
And he said, Sue me. What you
need's a berry bush or two.
The robin in the arbor nearby
said, My wisdom
is quotidian existence.
And the corgi in the backyard
on the other side barked, Me,
just speaking for myself,
I think I'll roll in shit.

PAN, TRACK, ZOOM

And he shall be like a tree planted by the rivers
of water, that bringeth forth his fruit in his
season.   Psalm 1

The wind from the lake releases
pollen over the tasseling corn,
while wreckage underwater slips
below the light. The sun
retreats into the great room
of his sister stars gone west,
and a fig wasp steps inside a fig.

WITHOUT A WORD

I answered thee in the secret place of thunder.
Psalm 81

When lightning flung us
out of the dark
where we lay face to face,
the searching looks
which had been hidden
met without a word. Then,
dark again. Then, thunder.

LESSON FOR PIANOFORTE:
THE BRAIN TUMOR

*None of the men of might have found their
hands.*   Psalm 76

His left hand weightless
on the keyboard
made no sound, no more
than cobwebs rending
under the freight of dust.

THE FREEDOM OF THE BODYSURFER

Thou shalt make them drink of the river of thy
pleasures.   Psalm 36

Swept up, free, borne up, to ride the wave—
not slammed down into the shingle, not hauled
under, breathless, struck flat face-first
into the gravel, not dragged no breath yet
still scrambling under churned foam frantic
to break water, gristle in one shoulder snapped,
no gasp, no burst of air yet, yet not drowning,
not yet, no—to ride the wave, as if forever
free, to breathe, to fill with air this rib cage
made to drink of the river of thy pleasures . . .

OLEH LYSHEHA RECEIVES HIS PRIZE

I will open my mouth in a parable: I will utter
dark sayings of old.   Psalm 78

Oleh Lysheha, Ukrainian poet,
stood at the podium, solemn.
I am an old man, he said.
He looked fifty, listeners silent.
I am an old man, he repeated.

Later, he told me, he would be
a long month in the woods.
It will be like a hundred years,
he said. I am a snake.
You know, the snakes that find
the little animals by heat?

Pit vipers.

          Yes, these. Only:
I come out of the stars.

THE PASSION OF COLIC

Out of the mouth of babes . . .   Psalm 8

Putting herself to sleep,
she screams: she needs our help
to stop. The doctor said
we could ignore her screams
and she'd pass out. But chaos roars
through the apartment, which is small.

The moon is tiny although full, the stars
funereally mum. You may wish
to think of them as heaven.
You may fume at what makes you
feel helpless in her scream.
Praises of the excellences of this world

may not come to mind. But we had better
pray at any rate, though in our thoughts
we curse her, and ourselves,
and for his longtime unforgiving absence
God—pray: let that baby rage; let not
one muscle wrenching me with anger budge.

I WANT TO PRAY

In the hidden part thou shalt make me to know wisdom.   Psalm 51

That young man
firing his Kalashnikov
into the playground
has been made to know
the hidden part.

Me, I want to pray.
I'm on my knees.
But all I am is screaming
I don't know what for. Maybe
the best God can do is pay no mind.

MONSTER MINDED

Thou hast made us to drink the wine of astonishment.
Psalm 60

The wine of astonishment
is house wine at my house.
The whiskey of it is a sauce
we savor. The cocaine
of thy judgment also
is rock crystal, blow
to blow the mitral valve.
Truly is the heroin
of thine excellency said
to be deep brown, shit
pure enough to stop the heart.

THREE LILIES

Weeping may endure for a night, but joy cometh in the morning.   Psalm 30

Before dawn, under a thin moon disappearing
east, the planet Mercury, the messenger
and healer, came up vanishingly
into the blue beyond the garden where
three lilies at the bottom of the yard
arrayed white trumpets on iron stalks
under a slow, slow lightning from the sun.
I stood on a rotten step myself,
and smelled them from a hundred feet away.

ON SECOND THOUGHT

It is he that hath made us, and not we ourselves.
Psalm 100

The infinite, though inconceivable to us,
is not, therefore, the superhero in a myth.
It's math. And zero is mathematically a fact.
Science so far indicates a zero set of gods
in this infinity. Me, godforsaken as I am,
I think God never did exist to go away.
This makes my godforsakenness complete.
It could be no greater and no less.

OPPOSITIONAL

They set their mouth against the heavens, and their tongue walketh through the earth . . . And they say, How doth God know? Psalm 73

After a thunderstorm
the front page, rain-soaked,
tears under its own weight
when you peel it free.

God, just so, has lifted up
and read my mind,
the print on both sides
visible at once.

THE SUICIDE OF
FRANCESCO BORROMINI

*Except the Lord build the house, they labour in vain
that build it.*   Psalm 127

The snail that wound himself a sleeve of pearl
could not have doubted much, as Borromini did,
who thought that he had failed, and hid himself,
and fell for shame, an old man, on his sword.
But first he built, not quite the way his father had,
with mason's chisel and a solid back; yet, hands
gone soft, he did lift great stones into shapes
no one but he, Francesco, could have seen. He made
stone yet unquarried levitate into eccentric domes,
with scalloped architraves, and towers, pinnacled
and crocketed and finialed with spheres. Builder
of three houses for the saints in Rome, he did what
all the saints agreed, unshriven, would mean hell,
then made confession, dying, and received last rites.

I FORGOT

I said in my haste, All men are liars.   Psalm 116

I forgot to say, about the women,
they're all liars too. Children,
no one knows why, tell the truth,
but just enough to make the men
and women laugh. The words
we breathe are smoke. The living
wood inside the fire burns
and is not burned. It says, I am.

SNOWFALL, CHILDREN AT THEIR WINDOW

I laid me down and slept; I awaked; for the Lord
sustained me.   Psalm 3

Snowfall came in everybody's sleep
like sheets of lightning torn
from memory into strips
and shredded, frayed and dropped.
Snow every day, and every day
even to fear death is surprising.

WHAT SHE THINKS OF HOW I DRESS

*Hide not thy face far from me; put not thy servant
away in anger.*   Psalm 27

My wool shirts, put away for twenty years,
look bright red still, bright blue. It's creepy
they're so bright. I wear them in the attic
at my desk, where nothing could be creepier,
or better kept, than anger is in me. My wife
keeps telling me I look ridiculous. Unmarried
Schopenhauer (and I translate freely) saw
in God the angriest imaginable fuck. Freud,
forever angry with his wife, asked once
in print what women want. I want (in anger,
in my garret, which was the servant's quarters,
in the blue shirt that smells mightily of dust
and cedar) want: to pray: Hide thou neither thee
nor me. Let me feel what love I need to ask.

JADWIGA

I am forgotten as a dead man out of mind; I am like
a broken vessel.   Psalm 31

The feet of the servant's bed left scars
in the deck paint. In an otherwise raw
attic sixty years ago, for her, the room
with cardboard walls, with simulated
woodgrain finish, kept out February cold
about as well as an old appliance box,
appropriate, since *she* was old. She looked
old anyway, at my age, forty-eight.
For me, the room has insulation, storms,
my desk where her bed was. When I showed it
just now to an old man who'd come back
to see his childhood home, he said his nurse,
Jadwiga, nights when she could see her breath here
under the bare bulb, prayed for him, and slept.

MISERERE

Thou tellest my wanderings: put thou my tears into
thy bottle: are they not in thy book?   Psalm 56

Angels who came to us
where she lay supine, weeping,
stooped with their syringes
to the corners of her eyes
and drew these drops.

ROTGUT

The sun shall not smite thee by day, nor the moon by night.   Psalm 121

On a hillside scattered with temples broken
under the dog-day sun, my friend and I drank
local wine at nightfall and ate grape leaves
in goat-yogurt glaze. The living grape vines
bore fruit overhead. Beyond our balcony,
beyond the Turkish rooftops, an old moon
touched Venus at one tip. This vintage,
he said, would melt pig iron. But I wondered,
were we drunk enough, and he said no. I took him,
staggering and laughing, in my arms, and soon,
with snow at nightfall easing off,
another old moon slid into the hill
behind my dead friend's house. He loved
that smear of light cast back on it from earth.

BEWILDERED

He is like the beasts that perish.   Psalm 49

His skin like silk upon first kneeling ripped
between his knee bones and the little rocks.
The king on all fours flinching bit
into the tenderest shoot of a thistle.
Less with shame than with dumb relief, he felt
his palms and fingers, after their lifetime's
lingering on flax and cotton, thrill
at the jeweled edges of hot grit.

HOLINESS

*Thus they changed their glory into the similitude of
an ox that eateth grass.*   Psalm 106

God changed his glory into the very image
of a woman who ate snails and crème brûlée.
She worked her glory into an actual hootchie-koo,
while roosters crowed the day loose from the dark.

SCHIZOPHRENIC

*My wounds stink and are corrupt because of my
foolishness.*   Psalm 38

Foolish though I am, I have no wounds.
Let's not exaggerate. My sores stink
from the filth dried in my clothes.
God chooses this for me. *The mouth
of them that speak lies shall be stopped.*

MAKERS

He that formed the eye, shall he not see?   Psalm 94

What made us
come snapped shut
our eyes.

GOD'S WORLD, 1927

After the flood spilled over the sandbags on the levee,
each bag placed where one was needed burst. The bags
weighed half what men did. Men kept filling them

and carrying them uphill, to be set where now they burst
that instant. All night, in a freezing downpour, poor
white men with pistols, shivering and cursing, had made

black men, sharecroppers and convicts, tote the bags.
The few men shot dead running washed away. Others
were prevailed upon to sing. They sang in praise

of outlaws and of God. To the west a big uprooted
cottonwood raked over the underwater tops of willows.
Dawn. East, thirty feet below flood crest stood shacks

and mansions. Black men (hundreds, freezing, muscles
aching, hurt) and white men (holding them at gunpoint),
all, could feel foretremblings in the ground

about to be pushed out from under them. They saw,
at seven-thirty, Thursday, April twenty-first, the wall
of earth come open. Then, the cataclysm (with nobody-knows-

how-many men) broke over the fields where tall pecan trees
snapped, shacks tumbled, shattered, mules screamed.
And the psalm says, Be ye lift up, ye everlasting doors.

REDHEAD

He shall cover thee with his feathers.   Psalm 91

Through the snowdrift, mewing,
purring, comes the rufous-headed male
who, were she Lakshmi, would be Vishnu,
dancers into being of a duckly cosmos:
Fred and Ginger. When she spreads
her wings to warm us, how my mind goes
white with the scent of down and snowflakes!

JUSTICE

I am shut up, and I cannot come forth ... Wilt
thou show wonders to the dead?   Psalm 88

God flung me into the lowest pit.
In darkness he forgot my soul.
He no more shows me love than makes
dead tongues to speak. His wrath
has left me hideous with pain.
I have no lover, and no friend. You
(who hear me cry, who say that God
is with me even now in hell)
be damned, and see who cares.

INMATES

A man in isolation for three years
did push-ups all day, hundreds at a pop.
Between the lockup and the shower,
snapping the shackles at his wrists,
he took two guards and broke
their necks, then, with a shiv
another inmate handed him, beheaded
one, and waved the head, and roared.
In their cells the hellchoir
sang with him a song of life
in maximum security without parole.

SEAMLESS

*In the hidden part thou shalt make me to know
wisdom.*   Psalm 51

Sparks from amidbrain surge
on threads into the forelobe
where I think I smell shampoo
and back in a sweep of firings
into the hindbrain where I see her.
Over the cortex riddled by her
whisper, by her touch, by words
and urges, scannings tweak my wits
ten times per second: quickening
then damping: timing the flow
so that the world in mind seems
seamless, so that her lower lip
tipped open by my forefinger now
blooms with a notion dawning
on her face, which cannot help
but show the lucid storm of thought
in which she knows I see her
see me see her being touched.

AUGHT-ONE: LEONIDS, PREDAWN

Shall thy wonders be known in the dark?   Psalm 88

Meteors kept slipping past the windshield,
fifty-mile-long streaks of white-hot flame.
On the outskirts, three men
stood beside their cars to watch.
Whatever brought us here
had brought all four of us alone.
I spread my lawn chair in a field,
pitch dark, with cold-night smell
of cow flop, and a yard dog barking
from across the road. The kitchen
light came on inside the farmhouse.
Plumes of dawn gray drifted
into the night sky over the hillside east,
and gables, walls, black shapes of trees
grew vaguely solid in the dark—
above these, meteors. At last,
beyond the pink and violet scud
where only the most brilliant, nearest
star, the Dog Star, was still visible,
a final white streak singed the blue,
and I plunged after it
into the thick of daylight.

FIRST TOUCH

She turned away, the flame
of attraction sombering
like a bruise. Her smile
came back, to my confusion,
angry, and she laid her palm
under my fifth rib, where I saw
she meant to hurt me.

METHINKS IT, ERGO EST

O Lord, thou hast searched me, and known me.
Psalm 139

The works and workings of the mind
apart from God are covertures
of nothing. God's name is: I am.
His saying so to me or Moses,
meanwhile, merely seems. *I think*
in English means I seem. *Methinks it*
means it seems to me, or it thinks me.
God thinks me when he says I am.
My name must be methinks, or so it seems.

HOOKAH OF BLOWN GLASS

For I am become like a bottle in the smoke.
Psalm 119

Glass made green by a trace of iron flows
  in the walls of the bottle downward, drawn
    to the iron core of the planet,
      which is a ball afloat in a molten sphere.
Tiny bubbles captured in the glass drift
under the brush of light from a half-moon in the pinetop.
  Smoke from the crumbs of hashish, pulled
    through a long reed underwater, bursts
      behind the blue-green glass
        into a trail of smoky, wobbling spheres.
The moon and the iron tug at the smoke
  while the cloud in the bottle
rushes into the loops of the tube between my lips
    to swirl with resin past my teeth and tongue,
  to sink in my windpipe, sink, and sunken, hang.
Smoke hangs in the little pockets inside my lungs
  where the tiniest threads of blood
    are woven together into the thinnest walls.
Smoked blood spills back into my pumping heart,
  and when I feel smoke floating in my brain,
    I am become like a bottle in the smoke.

HIERARCHIES FOR THE PRAISE OF GOD

About the order of the groups
the squabble must have gone like this:
the singers said, We praise God
in God's words, which he vouchsafed
us only. Everyone loves fanfare,
but the keepers of God's
very word should enter first
and be the last to go. Players
should be persons of slight stature,
playing less loud this time,
please, and maybe they could wear
white robes with not quite so much
gold around the hem. Listen!
one of the players said, God's
music apprehends the very mind
of God as manifest most wholly
in the minds of men: it is not mere
traffic in whichever word drops
next with sputum from the lips
of the unclean. The damsels
laughed, and pointed out
that singers, players, and suchlike
were slaves who would do well
to walk precisely where the damsels

said and not distract the gentler
minds at court from the immaculate
procession of their virgin limbs.
The wisdom of the damsels proved,
in fact, to be the will of God.

FISTS I THOUGHT WERE MADE
TO HOLD THE REINS

He delighteth not in the strength of the horse . . .
He maketh peace . . .   Psalm 147

Catfish, lacking scales, are beautiful
in their repulsive way, but they will give you
an infected wound if you're not careful.
The filets I rubbed with cayenne, chili, salt,
and ginger, skillet hot and dry, then drowned
with lemon. Even the kids, who don't eat fish,
left none. My wife and I stopped brooding,
and my right hand opened with me staring
into the empty palm, long having, if I ever
knew, forgotten when and how the reins
slipped free. I love equestrians,
but I let go the reins, unlike my heroes,
lacking their authority, and wishing now
to lack my lack as well. An unimaginable horse
is rippling at a gallop far away, unshod,
with hoofbeats as impermanent as stars.

SACKCLOTH

*I made sackcloth also my garment; and I became a
proverb to them. They that sit in the gate speak
against me; and I was the song of the drunkards.*
Psalm 69

I made sackcloth my garment once, by cutting
arm and neck holes into a burlap bag.
A croker sack, they called it. Sackdragger,
they called the man who dragged a croker sack
between the cotton rows to pick. He dragged
a gunnysack behind him in the ditch
collecting empties. Him they chose
the Likeliest to Sack Seed in the feed store,
or to suck seed. He was your daddy. He
sacked groceries part-time. And they jeered:
you sorry sack of shit. Sackcloth,
which Job sewed upon his skin, was goat hair.
God who clothed the heavens with such blackness
said, I make sackcloth their covering.
Isaiah understood. God had him speak a word
in season to the weary. Speak, Isaiah, now, to me.
Before the stars like green figs in a windstorm
drop, the sun is black as sackcloth, and the moon
becomes as blood. My soul is weary. Speak,
Isaiah. Sing. I was a scholar as a boy:
I cut the neck and arm holes into the burlap,
pulled it on, and cinched it with a hank of rope:
what I have done from then till now is itch.

AT THE BLACK HOLE WHERE THE SALMON RIVER REELS AND PLUNGES WEST

I am poured out like water.   Psalm 22

The monsters having spawned now wait,
that sheen on some a window smashed
and fogged inside by bruises
from sideswiping rock.
Leaves from cliff walls
rusting in September
flake and fall away
downwind, downstream,
and under, cloudcombs
in the blue of the early dark.

AMOR FATI

*How amiable are thy tabernacles, O Lord of
hosts! . . . The rain also filleth the pools.*   Psalm 84

How amiably dirt has filled the breadth of my front yard!
I step there without hurtling into the black hole
at the center of the Milky Way. Because two amiable
haploid cells have filled my body also with myself,
I see air filled with air where light is filling
light with light. Birdsongs pierce my longing
with sharp hints, how largely largeness fills the small!

PSALM 133, QUOTED IN FULL

Behold, how good and how pleasant it is for brethren
to dwell together in unity!

It is like the precious ointment upon the head, that
ran down upon the beard, even Aaron's beard: that went down
to the skirts of his garments;

As the dew of Hermon, and as the dew that descended
upon the mountains of Zion: for there the Lord commanded
his blessing, even life for evermore.

GLOSS

He shall come down like rain upon the mown grass.
Psalm 72

One collector of the psalms
in Hebrew says the wise king
sings this psalm about himself;
translators into the Greek say,
No, the father prophesies
the greatness of his son; some
in Aramaic say the good king
praised here as a king of kings
would be the One Annointed;
psalm and commentaries, all
from unknown hands, descend
through centuries like rain.
Into the living mind, out of a cloud
of hands, these blessings fall,
like rain upon the mown grass.

OF THE NUMBER LIVING

They that sow in tears shall reap in joy. Psalm 126

More than a billion heads swim, some
with several faiths at once, in hunger.
Half a billion sow in tears, malarial,
or syphilitic, leprous, faces
split with yaws. The truly starving
may not reap, but they that sow in tears
most often reap in tears. This psalm
says, The Lord hath done great things.

FLOOD WITH GAR, 1973

*Whatsoever passeth through the paths of the
seas ...*   Psalm 8

She saw them from the causeway, rolling
over the flooded bean fields, gar
with hearts as big as men's, and scales
so hard a well-aimed butcher's blade
would just make sparks and glance away.
A thousand years ago, the tribe
who raised the pyramids of earth nearby,
and built their temples at the top,
used gar scales for their arrowheads.
Then, all at once, their temples burned.
Why, no one knows. The road dipped.
Over a sandbag wall she saw
a bobcat swimming just about
eye-level with the flood and her.

OATH

*Set a watch, O Lord, before my mouth; keep the door
of my lips.*   Psalm 141

Winding down, for want of respite
from the never-endingly untrue, breast pocket
empty, where my forefinger shows God
to aim, I say: These lies *are* true. No:
cross my heart, so help me, hope to die.

MEDLEY
Lines from Psalms 142–149

Bring my soul out of prison, that I may praise thy name.
My soul thirsteth after thee, as a thirsty land. Selah.
Hide not thy face. Cause me to hear thy lovingkindness.
I will sing a new song unto thee, O God: upon a psaltery
and an instrument of ten strings will I sing praises unto thee.
The Lord is gracious, and full of compassion; slow to anger,
and of great mercy. Put not your trust in princes,
nor in the son of man, in whom there is no help. Great
is the Lord. He casteth forth his ice like morsels;
who can stand before his cold? Praise the Lord from the earth,
ye dragons, and all deeps. Praise his name in the dance:
let them sing praises unto him with the timbrel and harp.

ONE TEAR

Thy judgments are a great deep.   Psalm 36

One tear not yet large enough to spill,
upwelling at the corner of an eye, may
delve with a root of salt inside the tongue,
and shimmer of it thrown among the stars go
lightyears. Deeper art thou far beyond all
shimmer in thy fathom, Father, O thou
mindless, in the furthering of thy judgment.

COMMUTER FLIGHT

Fire, and hail; snow, and vapour; stormy wind
fulfilling his word.   Psalm 148

Last night's snow inside the cloud
roared past my window,
big flakes dry with cold, night
calm. Drifts floodlit
on the interstate swam
in and out of focus underneath.
We landed on the tarmac
below zero, quiet,
glad to be lukewarm
on the frozen earth.

DEAF

Deep calleth unto deep at the noise of thy
waterspouts.   Psalm 42

The waterfall in sunlight is God
talking to herself. Her voice
poured into the trees asks
nothing, to prove nothing,
and her way of asking
says by overflowing what
may not be said. The stream
unbroken at the rock's
edge bursts with downflung
beads where daylight bursts
and drops. Though deaf, I listen
through my shoe-soles, through
the stone ledge, into the water,
thrumming, into the spray and light.

I LOVE TO SEE GOD

He looketh on the earth, and it trembleth: he
toucheth the hills, and they smoke.   Psalm 104

I love to see God, clothed with light as with a garment,
carpentering beams of balconies under a cosmic sea
and clothing them to their foundation with his deeps
as with a garment, too. This psalm, and most of them,
my mother's mother had by heart. Forgetful, I read
out loud from her husband's Bible: I will sing praise
to my God while I have my being. My father's mother's
people sang in Hebrew, words with tunes their forebears
kept in mind, how many generations?—three-, four-
score. Maybe I'm dreaming. I may wake up yet,
and sing praise of my birthright in their tongue.

SCROLLS

So will I compass thine altar, O Lord: That I may
publish with the voice of thanksgiving. Psalm 26

Thine altar is to me this bathtub
where my four-year-old twin
girls tip back their heads.
They close their eyes.
I read their faces from above,
in trust and fear, in holiness,
heads tipped until the waterline
has touched their hairlines, cautious.
Look: their hair flows underwater
like the scrolls unfurled in heaven.

IN THIS LIFE, WE WAIT

My soul waiteth for the Lord more than they that
watch for the morning: I say, more than they that
watch for the morning.   Psalm 130

Isaiah's watchman cried out, Babylon
is fallen. Fallen, he said, broken,
all her graven images. Out of the wilderness
another voice came, Watchman, what of the night?
And the watchman, leaning from his tower,
cried, The morning cometh, also the night.

MISSAL

*Praise him upon the loud cymbals: praise him upon
the high sounding cymbals.*   Psalm 150

I set these words beside the wind chime rusting in its box.

Notes

3   "Submersible": My main source for details of deep-sea exploration is
     William Broad's *The Universe Below.*

5   *"Apollo 12":* The astronaut in the photograph is Al Bean, on the second
     lunar landing, in November 1969.

6   "Thy Name": Dr. Charles Talbut Onions was the last editor of the original
     Oxford English Dictionary and the principal editor of the posthumously
     published *Oxford Dictionary of English Etymology.* In Dr. Onions's
     idiom, his personal copy of the eighteenth-century *Dictionary of the
     English Language* was his Johnson. According to an old tradition—
     discredited by Luther and subsequent scholars—King Solomon, the son of
     King David the Psalmist, wrote Ecclesiastes, the most thoroughly skeptical
     book in Hebrew scripture. It is the source of two quotes here, about the
     fool and about time and chance. Verses cited in this poem besides Psalm 22
     are John 1:1, Genesis 1:27, Psalms 14:1, and Ecclesiastes 9:11 and 2:15.

7   "Wedding Song": The king's chief musician, singing Psalm 45 in honor of
     the royal couple, warns the foreign bride, apparently as part of his
     commission: "forget also thine own people, and thy father's house." The
     queen, singing for herself in this antiphony, urges the king to remember.
     The queen of Sheba, who paid tribute to King Solomon (1 Kings 10), and
     Jezebel the Chaste, who persuaded King Ahab to build an altar to the
     god Baal (1 Kings 16), are queens of gentile descent whom this psalm
     calls to mind.

9   "Unclean": The poem by Giacomo Leopardi is *Passero solitario*, or "Solitary Sparrow."

10   "Dark": During the plague of darkness, the Egyptians "saw not one another . . . but all the children of Israel had light in their dwellings" (Exodus 10:23).

11   "I Woke Up and It Was Time": In general, the best time to observe meteors is between midnight and dawn, when the atmosphere overhead is turning more and more fully toward the particles in the path of Earth's orbit. The meteor showers that occur in mid-August of each year, when Earth is passing through the remnants of Comet 1862 III, are called Perseids, because the meteors appear to radiate from the constellation Perseus. The display in August 2001, expected by some astronomers to be more conspicuous than usual, was not.

12   "Every Death Is Magic from the Enemy to Be Avenged": For people who believe that death within the tribe is always magic perpetrated by the enemy, all deaths require vengeance. In these religions, the cold-blooded murder of women and children from enemy tribes may be considered a sacred duty. Such magical thinking seems to permeate all war.

13   "1985": Much of my sense of the air war in Vietnam comes from Jonathan Schell's *The Military Half*.

14   "Kingliness": Shakespeare's presentation of King Richard III as "deform'd" and inhuman is an exaggeration drawn from chroniclers working under the Tudor dynasty. The Tudors, who took the throne from the house of York by killing Richard, made their bloody ascent appear less awful by painting Richard as a monster. Historians correcting this account are said to have "rehabilitated" Richard, although nearly everyone agrees that he made his way to the throne by murdering whoever interfered with his succession, including his own brother and his two young nephews.

15   "Praise Ye Him": The First Book of Samuel records David's rise to power and his troubles with King Saul, including the attempts on David's life when "the Spirit of the Lord departed from Saul, and an evil spirit from the Lord troubled him" (1 Samuel 16:14, 18:10, and 19:9). The story casts a revealing sidelight on the Psalms regarded as King David's legacy, songs

preoccupied with kings and kingdoms, enemies and bloodshed. Verses quoted here include Saul's reference to his daughter Michal as a "snare" in 1 Samuel 19:21, and the words said to have been sung by David, in Psalms 58:7 and 10, 59:17, 68:23, and 72:9.

20   "The Freedom of the Bodysurfer": Irresistible power seems implicit in the phrase "thy pleasures," as when "at thy pleasure" means "according to thy will." The ironic overtones of this phrase in English do not occur in the original Hebrew.

23   "I Want to Pray": Mikhail Kalashnikov, whose ingeniously simple design made the AK-47 the most numerous assault rifle in the world, died an old man, of natural causes. As Thomas Lux said in his disturbing poem about this weapon, "everybody's got one."

24   "Monster Minded": Like "the dregs of the cup of my fury" ("the cup of trembling") in Isaiah, 51:17 and 22, "the wine of astonishment" in Psalm 60 represents the horrors of war.

28   "The Suicide of Francesco Borromini": Architect and sculptor Francesco Borromini, 1599–1667, was Giovanni Bernini's greatest contemporary. Early in their careers the two of them collaborated on Saint Peter's. After that, Bernini, the more socially adroit, became more celebrated and successful. Borromini, the more reclusive, suffered from mania and depression and had more and more difficulty securing the support he needed to finish his projects.

29   "I Forgot": Moses encounters the burning bush in the third chapter of Exodus.

31   "What She Thinks of How I Dress": In 1936, on Freud's eightieth birthday in Vienna, Thomas Mann delivered a lecture, "Freud and the Future," in which he compared the will and intellect in Schopenhauer's cosmos to the id and ego in Freud's psyche.

32   "Jadwiga": In 1386, when the marriage of the twelve-year-old Polish Princess Jadwiga to the grand duke of Lithuania had united the last nation of pagans in Europe with the Catholic kingdom of Poland, the Lithuanian people submitted to a mass baptism on their riverbanks. Since then,

Jadwiga has been a popular girl's name in Poland, associated with the saintliness of the famous princess. Czeslaw Milosz refers to this history in his memoir, *Native Realm*.

35   "Bewildered": After King Nebuchadnezzar's army had demolished the temple in Jerusalem in 586 B.C.E., he came to revere the God of Israel, whose people were by then his people's slaves. Toward the end of his life, the king protected the Israelites, and he was prosperous and happy. First, though, according to the Book of Daniel 4:33, Nebuchadnezzar "was driven from men, and did eat grass as oxen, and his body was wet with the dew of heaven, till his hairs were grown like eagles' feathers, and his nails like birds' claws."

37   "Schizophrenic": The last sentence of this poem is quoted from Psalms 63:11.

39   "God's World, 1927": Many details about the flood of 1927 come from John Barry's excellent account, *Rising Tide*. The last line here is from the seventh verse of Psalm 24.

41   "Redhead": According to the Peterson guide, the redhead drake meows and purrs. Typically, the drake leaves the hen during incubation, and the hen leaves the young before they fledge. Unseasonal snowstorms such as the one in this poem may occur in the breeding range of this species.

42   "Justice": This poem paraphrases Psalm 88, which is widely regarded as the most despairing poem in scripture.

44   "Seamless": For thinking about how separate faculties seated in various regions of the brain may be integrated into a single "seamless" consciousness, my main source is Robert A. Lavine's *Neurophysiology*, the textbook my wife happened to use in medical school. The notion of seamlessness echoes the description of Joseph's famous coat as one "without a seam," a phrase implying in Hebrew that the seams have disappeared. The last lines here recast a phrase from Steven Pinker's book about computational and evolutionary models of consciousness, *How the Mind Works*.

45   "Aught-One: Leonids, Predawn": The meteor showers that occur in mid-November of each year, when Earth is passing through the remnants

of Comet 1866 I, are called Leonids, because the meteors appear to radiate from the constellation Leo. The display on November 19, 2001, was, as predicted, the most vivid since 1966. (See also the note on "I Woke Up and It Was Time.")

46   "First Touch": In Second Samuel—which records the reign of King David the Psalmist—and nowhere else in scripture, mortal blows are reported in several cases to have been struck to "the fifth rib," the rib over the heart.

48   "Hookah of Blown Glass": What the King James calls "a bottle in the smoke" is a bag, a waterskin or wineskin, in the Hebrew. To invert this image, and to picture the smoke in a bottle, suggested to my mind a hookah. Abandoning the sense of the psalm to dwell on the inversion of the English, the speaker sees himself as a fragile container for intoxicating smoke. This recalls Isaiah's phrase, "drunken, but not with wine," and the prose poem by Baudelaire, "It's always necessary to be drunk. On what? On wine, on poetry, or on virtue . . ."

49   "Hierarchies for the Praise of God": Because so much of this psalm, among others, concerns the subjugation of armies, princes, and kings, it takes only a slight perversity in the reader to think of the singers, players, and damsels also vying for position.

52   "Sackcloth": The word "sack," repeated several times in this poem, may have such pungency in English because it is so ancient and widespread. Almost identical cognates have existed in Hebrew, French, German, Gaelic, Russian, and related languages. Inflected forms occur in Assyrian, Greek, Latin, Old Norse, and others. Verses quoted here are: Job 16:15, Isaiah 50:3–4, and Revelations 6:12–3.

55   "Psalm 133, Quoted in Full": The spirit of this psalm is especially refreshing in the context of the Book of Psalms as a whole where, for example, the word "friend" is used only in connection with betrayal.

56   "Gloss": The sense of the composition, original text, use, and interpretation of Psalms in many of these poems, and especially in this one, draws on Artur Weis's *The Psalms*.

60   "Medley": This string of quotes is meant to dwell, with the rest of these antiphonies, on the tension in thought and feeling between skepticism and

devotion. Scholars believe that the Hebrew word *selah* is a piece of musical notation, which may indicate a rise in pitch or volume, or a pause. Whatever shift it signals, clearly it invites a stronger response.

61   "One Tear": This poem and others echo lines by Hayden Carruth, in this case his great poem "Mother."

64   "I Love to See God": Psalm 104 is often called the most beautifully sustained song of praise in the Bible. This poem paraphrases lines near the beginning and toward the end of the psalm.

66   "In This Life, We Wait": The title, from Jean Valentine's poem "Juliana," echoes several psalms besides 130. The passage about the watchman, quoted and paraphrased here, is in the twenty-first chapter of Isaiah.

Acknowledgments

The author thanks the editors of the following publications where poems from this book appeared, some in slightly different form.

Georgia Review: "I Woke Up and It Was Time," "Aught-One: Leonids, Predawn"

Hammer and Blaze: a Gathering of Contemporary American Poets (University of Georgia Press, 2002): "Submersible," "I AM," "Sackcloth," "God's World, 1927," "Rotgut," "Scrolls"

New England Review: "Submersible"

Ontario Review: "Without a Word," *"Amor Fati,"* "Justice," "Kindness"

Paris Review: "Hierarchy," *"Apollo 12,"* "One Tear"

Partisan Review: "I AM"

Sundog: "The Suicide of Francesco Boromini"

Turnrow: "Thy Name," "Unclean," "Every Death Is Magic from the Enemy to Be Avenged," "1985," "Monster Minded," "I Want to Pray," "Rotgut," "Sackcloth"

Virginia Quarterly: "On Second Thought," "I Love to See God"

Yale Review: "Deaf"

Thanks to Deborah Garrison, my editor at Knopf, for the friendliness of her guiding intelligence; and to her assistant, Ilana Kurshan, for her help and enthusiasm. Friends who offered detailed comments in response to drafts have helped improve these poems, though they share no part of the responsibility for my shortcomings: Mary Karr, Susan Kolodny, Joe-Anne McLaughlin, Daniel Moriarty, and Andy Robbins. The warmth of Ken Frieden's interest, as a scholar and an artist, in this poor man's midrash was a decisive support. Above all, thanks to my children, Hebrew scholars all; my wife, who has steered them and me in that direction; and to the rest of my family.

A Note About the Author

Brooks Haxton is the son of novelist Ellen Douglas and composer Kenneth Haxton. He has published two book-length narrative poems, four previous collections of poetry, and translations of Victor Hugo, Heraclitus, and selected poems from the ancient Greek. He has received awards and fellowships from the National Endowment for the Arts and the John Simon Guggenheim Foundation, among others. He lives with his wife and three children in Syracuse, and teaches at the Syracuse University Program in Creative Writing and the Warren Wilson MFA Program for Writers.

A Note on the Type

The text of this book was set in a typeface called Aldus, designed by the celebrated typographer Hermann Zapf in 1952–1953. Based on the classical proportion of the popular Palatino type family, Aldus was originally adapted for Linotype composition as a slightly lighter version that would read better in smaller sizes. Hermann Zapf was born in Nuremburg, Germany, in 1918. He has created many other well known typefaces including Comenius, Hunt Roman, Marconi, Melior, Michelangelo, Optima, Saphir, Sistina, Zapf Book, and Zapf Chancery.

Composed by Creative Graphics,
Allentown, Pennsylvania
Printed and bound by United Book Press,
Baltimore, Maryland
Designed by Anthea Lingeman